Why lose your temper?

By Janine Amos and Annabel Spenceley
Consultant Rachael Underwood

CHERRYTREE BOOKS

A Cherrytree Book

Designed and produced by A S Publishing
Design and typesetting by James Leaman and Michael Leaman

First published 2000
by Cherrytree Press
327 High Street
Slough
Berkshire
SL1 1TX

A subsidiary of the Evans Publishing Group

British Library Cataloguing in Publication Data
Amos, Janine
Why lose your temper? – (Problem solvers)
1. Temper. Juvenile Literature
I. Title II. Spenceley, Annabel
302. 5'4

ISBN 1 842 34024 7

Printed in Italy by G. Canale & C. S.p.A. - Turin

Why lose your temper?

Sometimes you may get really angry. It can be frightening to feel angry. It can be scary for other people too.

Angry outbursts may be a problem for you and your friends but you can learn to deal with feeling angry. Here are some steps to help you.

 First of all, notice how you feel and try to tell people

 If you feel really angry, you will need an adult to help you

 Talk about the problem together

 Decide how to sort out the problem so that you feel better

The children in this book sort out their problems with the help of their teacher. As you read, see if you can follow the problem-solving steps they use.

Tom's Temper

Tom is building a space station. He gets more and more bricks. Up and up they go, into a huge tower.
  The tower begins to lean.

Tom makes the tower even higher. He watches the top bend over. Will it be strong enough?

Tom bites his lip.

The space station tumbles down. Tom is angry.

Tom smashes the model with his fist. He knocks
all the bricks off the table. He kicks one brick right
across the room.

Mrs Casey comes over to Tom.

"Hey!" she says, "I can see you're angry. But I can't let you do that. Someone might get hurt."

Tom says nothing.

"You look really angry, Tom," Mrs Casey goes on. "Your face is all red. You look as if you'll burst. Why not give me the brick."

Tom holds on to the brick. He is shaking. "I want to throw it," he says.

"You're so angry that you want to throw the brick,"
says Mrs Casey. "What else could you do that wouldn't
hurt anyone?"

Tom can't think.
"You could kick the big cushion," Mrs Casey tells him.

Mrs Casey leads Tom to the big cushion. Tom puts down the brick. He kicks the cushion over and over again.

Tom kicks and kicks the big cushion until he's kicked all the angry feelings out.

Skip to the Moon

Alice and Holly are in the playground. They both have new skipping ropes. They are skipping together, side by side, and counting their skips.

"Let's see who can do the most!" says Alice. "Let's have a competition!"

"OK," agrees Holly.

Alice goes first. Round and round goes the rope.
Holly counts, ". . . eighteen, nineteen, twenty!"
Alice has skipped twenty times. Her legs are tired.

Now it is Holly's turn. Alice sits and watches. She counts out loud for Holly.

Holly skips on and on. Alice stops counting.
"Twenty, twenty-one, TWENTY-TWO!" squeals Holly.
She has a big smile on her face.

Alice is shaking with anger. She stands up and throws her rope on the ground.

"I hate you!" shouts Alice at Holly.

"No you don't! You're just angry because you didn't win!" Holly tells her.

Mrs Casey hears the shouting. She hurries over.

"Alice is angry because I won the skipping," Holly tells her.

"I should have won!" sobs Alice. "I'm the best at skipping."

"You'd like to skip the most skips in the whole class?" says Mrs Casey.

"No, in the whole school," says Alice fiercely.

"How about in the whole country?" asks Mrs Casey.

"Or the whole world?" says Holly.

"I want to skip the most skips in the whole UNIVERSE!" says Alice.

"Let's skip to the moon together!" jokes Holly, and picks up Alice's rope.

"OK," laughs Alice, and takes the rope.

"Remember to come back for afternoon school!" calls Mrs Casey.

Side by side, Alice and Holly skip to the moon – and back!

When there's a problem

We all get angry sometimes. That's natural. Sometimes, though, our anger overpowers us and that can be frightening. We feel out of control. We lose our temper.

If you notice that someone is getting very angry, stop what you are doing. Call a teacher or another adult to help. If you are the one who is angry, try to remember:

DON'T hurt others
DON'T hurt yourself
DON'T damage things
DO talk about it

Problem Solving

Tom and Alice had problems with anger. Mrs Casey and their friends helped them solve the problems. If you are angry, here are some things you could do:

 Take some deep breaths

 Quietly count to ten, or twenty or a hundred

 Go to a place where you can feel calm – the book area or a quiet corner of the classroom or playground

 Let the anger out safely – run round the playground, kick a cushion, screw up lots of scrap paper and put it in the bin, draw an 'angry' picture

 Ask an adult for help